BRITAIN'S
KINGS & QUEENS

Michael St John Parker

Introduction

From Alfred the Great, in the ninth century, to Elizabeth II today, 56 very varied men and women have reigned as kings or queens of England. The royal line of Scotland merged with that of England only in the seventeenth century. Some of these sovereigns occupied the throne for no more than a few months or, like Henry VI and Edward IV, disputed its possession with a rival, and not all were formally crowned; others, such as Elizabeth I and Victoria, reigned in splendour for so long that they set the seal of their names on whole periods of history. Some were esteemed as saintly, some were conspicuously sinful, some were feared and strong, others were despised and weak.

The wide differences in personality of these kings and queens are matched by the variety of circumstances in which they reigned. The powers and the functions of a monarch of England have never ceased to evolve, the rules of succession have differed from one period of history to another, and the very extent of the kingdom has changed. So we must not imagine William

ABOVE: *Egbert, King of Wessex 802–839*. LEFT: *Alfred the Great's statue at Winchester, where he is buried.* OPPOSITE: *A coin of Cnut.*

the Conqueror wrangling with a Parliament, any more than we should imagine George III leading warriors into battle.

In fact, to go back to the beginnings of the British monarchy is to explore a landscape so different from the one in which we now live, that only the similarity of the place names allows us to assume that we are still in the same country. What we now call England was roughly carved up by immigrant Saxon war bands in the fifth and sixth centuries, to make tribal territories and principalities. Historians at one time liked to write of the Heptarchy – the Seven Kingdoms of Saxon England – but this was too neat a name for an untidy, constantly altering picture, in which powerful tribes inevitably conquered weaker ones, and then in turn went down before still greater neighbours. In the seventh century, the kingdom of Northumbria – the area north of a line between Humber and Ribble – led the other kingdoms in strength, wealth and cultural distinction; in the eighth century primacy passed to the midland kingdom of Mercia; while the ninth century saw the rise of Wessex, in the south.

It was the varied achievements of the rulers of Wessex that ultimately gave rise to the kingdom of England itself, with a royal house descended from the line of Alfred the Great.

Early Kings of Wessex

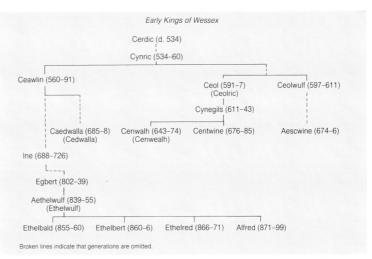

Early Kings of Wessex

```
                          Cerdic (d. 534)
                                |
                          Cynric (534–60)
            ┌───────────────────────────────────┬─────────────────────┐
      Ceawlin (560–91)                    Ceol (591–7)          Ceolwulf (597–611)
            |                              (Ceolric)
            |                                  |
            |                            Cynegils (611–43)
            |                ┌───────────────────────┬──────────────────┐
   Caedwalla (685–8)   Cenwalh (643–74)      Centwine (676–85)    Aescwine (674–6)
    (Cedwalla)          (Cenwealh)
            |
       Ine (688–726)
            L╌╌╌┐
         Egbert (802–39)
              |
       Aethelwulf (839–55)
         (Ethelwulf)
     ┌────────────┬──────────────┬──────────────┐
Ethelbald (855–60)  Ethelbert (860–6)  Ethelred (866–71)  Alfred (871–99)
```

Broken lines indicate that generations are omitted.

The squabbles and struggles of the Saxon principalities already mentioned were overtaken in the ninth century by the onset of a new wave of invaders, the Viking marauders from Scandinavia, who began at this time to terrorise the coastal regions of all of western Europe. It was the Viking menace that forced successive kings of Wessex to fight for their lives, and to show powers of statesmanship which are distinctly influential even today in the organisation of local government.

The Northmen were too strong to be permanently repulsed, however, and some mingling of forces was inevitable in the long run. When the house of Wessex failed to produce an obvious, powerful heir to the throne in the early eleventh century, it was a Dane, Cnut (Canute), who was accepted by Saxons and Northmen alike. Similarly, when the succession was in dispute again fifty years later, in 1066, it was another adventurer of Scandinavian origin, William of Normandy, who made good by force his claim to the throne. Thus was achieved the merger of Saxon and Scandinavian elements that produced medieval England.

Later Saxon and Danish Kings

In their different ways Cnut and William were both interlopers, at least by what have come to be regarded, since the eighteenth century, as the rules of royal succession. However, this fact did not invalidate their kingship in the eyes of their contemporaries. When kings had to rule as well as reign, there were always questions of suitability and acceptability, which could not always be easily settled by the accident of heredity.

The Saxons recognised certain families as royal, but kings succeeded not merely by line of descent – they had to command the support of the leading families, and their claim was strengthened if they could prove that they had been 'designated' for the succession by their predecessors. Usually, these considerations combined to produce a clearly favoured candidate but sometimes there was room for disagreement, and then came the resort to arms. In a sense, this resort to arms persisted until the last succession contest – that between Jacobites and Hanoverians – had died away in the eighteenth century. The genealogies in this book, like most genealogies, are meant to show a single line of descent; they make no attempt to describe that great puzzle of history – what might have been.

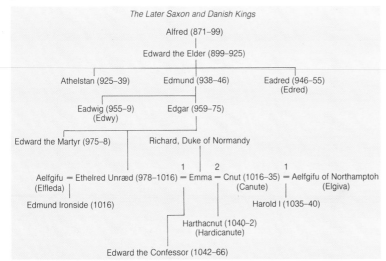

The Later Saxon and Danish Kings

```
                          Alfred (871–99)
                                |
                    Edward the Elder (899–925)
        ┌───────────────────────┬──────────────────────┐
 Athelstan (925–39)        Edmund (938–46)         Eadred (946–55)
                                |                    (Edred)
              ┌─────────────────┴────────┐
        Eadwig (955–9)              Edgar (959–75)
         (Edwy)
     ┌───────────┴──────────────┐
Edward the Martyr (975–8)   Richard, Duke of Normandy

                    1        2                      1
  Aelfgifu  =  Ethelred Unræd (978–1016)  =  Emma  =  Cnut (1016–35)  =  Aelfgifu of Northamptoh
  (Elfleda) |                                        (Canute)            (Elgiva)
            |
 Edmund Ironside (1016)                                      Harold I (1035–40)
                                |
                      Harthacnut (1040–2)
                       (Hardicanute)

            Edward the Confessor (1042–66)
```

Alfred the Great   871–899

Born 849
Buried Winchester

It is not possible to point to any one figure in the history of the English monarchy and say, simply, 'he – or she – began it all'. Nonetheless, the story did receive a tremendous, even a decisive, forward impulse from Alfred of Wessex, King of the English as he styled himself on his coins, and Leader of the Christians as he was called by his devoted biographer Asser. He is the only English ruler to have been popularly accepted as 'Great', and his position, both in British history as a whole and in the development of the monarchy in particular, is unique.

King Alfred's Jewel, which is supposed to have belonged to King Alfred. It is made of gold and enamel.

We know more about Alfred than about any other king of England before William the Conqueror, and the first features of his character to emerge are those of the warrior and the commander. Succeeding to the throne at a time when the Viking invasions were rising to a crescendo, Alfred had at one stage to struggle for bare survival but recovered to win his greatest victory in the field at Ethandune (Edington), in Wiltshire, where he routed a Danish army under King Guthrum, and subsequently compelled the survivors to capitulate at Chippenham and sign the peace of Wedmore (878). This successful campaign diminished the Viking threat, but could not remove it, and in the later part of his reign Alfred's role as an active soldier was less important than his work as a strategist and an architect of victory. He embarked on a programme of fortification to provide support for the local militia, whose organisation he strengthened. He also advanced his defensive frontiers by creating a naval force,

to patrol the coasts and meet invaders before they could deploy through the countryside. For this innovation, he is honoured as father of the Royal Navy.

The same quality of orginality that enabled Alfred to develop from a warrior into a military administrator inspired him to make his court in peacetime a centre of culture and religion worthy of European renown. His biographer, Asser, is full of admiration as he describes his hero:

'Meanwhile amid wars and the frequent hindrances of this present life, the incursions of the pagans and his own daily infirmities of body, the King did not cease to carry on the government and to engage in hunting of every form; to teach his goldsmiths and all his artificers, his falconers, hawkers and dog-keepers; to erect by his own inventive skill finer and more sumptuous buildings than had ever been the wont of his ancestors; to read aloud Saxon books, and above all, not only to command others to learn Saxon poems by heart but to study them himself in private to the best of his power. He also heard daily the divine office of the Mass, with certain psalms and prayers, and celebrated the canonical hours by day and night; and in the night he was wont to frequent the churches for prayers, secretly and without the knowledge of his court. He was a bountiful giver of alms, both to his own countrymen and to foreigners of all nations, incomparably affable and pleasant to all men, and a skilful investigator of the secrets of nature.'

Legislation and administration in the modern sense were not seen as significant parts of the duties of a Saxon king, but Alfred's general concern for the quality of life, and the breadth of his vision, were such that he was naturally led to codify and promulgate laws, and spend time dispensing justice — activities which thereby became for subsequent generations part of the expected activity of a good king.

Alfred was an avid collector of other men's talents; but he is still more remarkable in that he was

participant as well as patron in the culture of his brilliant court. He still speaks to us with amazing directness through his writings, most especially through his highly personal vernacular translations of Boethius and Augustine. It is from these, above all, that we feel we know him, as 'a man of strong imagination, anxious and temperamental; always afraid of himself, afraid of illness and incapacity to the point of hypochondria, aware of a larger world than he himself lived in, desperately keen to live in it, and to enable others to live in it.'

Edward the Elder   899–925

Born c.870
Crowned Kingston-upon-Thames
Buried Winchester

It was the custom of Saxon royal families that a king's sons should begin to share their father's duties as soon as they were capable of doing so, and Edward the Elder was commanding armies in battle and signing charters as 'Rex' some time before Alfred's death in 899. It is hardly surprising, then, to find him extending the pattern of Alfred's work, by pushing back further the Danish power and consolidating the structure of Saxon rule. But the chroniclers who described his achievements make it plain that much of the credit must go to Edward's older sister, Aethelflaed, who was married to the ruler of Mercia and seems to have governed that kingdom in her own right after her husband died in 910. Evidently a forceful, even a formidable woman, 'the lady of Mercia' campaigned on equal terms with her brother, and between them they inflicted a series of crushing defeats on the Danish settlers of the Midlands and East Anglia.

Aethelflaed died in 917, almost at the moment when the Danes of the Midlands made their final submission. Edward, who has been described as 'a formidable engine of war, a sort of infallible military machine which gets through its task with admirable accuracy, if not always with great speed', went on to extract oaths and submissions from the eastern and northern Danes as well.

The towns of Mercia were

systematically fortified to provide stability in defence, as Alfred had first taught in Wessex. Edward was probably also responsible for a new division of territories, on a military basis, which survived until recently, almost unaltered, in the county map of Midland England.

Like his father, Edward seems to have been more than just a soldier and administrator. He 'used books frequently', and his reign is notable for the beauty and originality of its coinage, in which he appears to have taken a direct interest. One of his portrait coins, in particular, is regarded as the finest thing to have been produced by an English mint until the reign of Edward I.

Athelstan   925–939

Born c.895
Crowned Kingston-upon-Thames
Buried Malmesbury

The royal house of Wessex reached a peak of splendour and success in the reign of Athelstan, one of the greatest warriors, administrators and patrons of art to occupy the English throne in the early medieval period. He consolidated the union of Wessex and Mercia, fastened a steadily tightening grip on Northumbria, which had long been under Danish control, received the homage of the princes of Wales, and justified his claim to the proud title *Rex Totius Britanniae* – King of all Britain – in the epic battle of Brunanburh. The precise site of this victory cannot be identified, but it was probably on the shores of the Solway Firth. Here, in 937, Athelstan crushed a confederation of Irish, Scottish and Norse warlords, before going on to subdue Scotland. Contemplating this triumph, the scribe of the Anglo-Saxon Chronicle was inspired to burst into exultant poetry in celebration of

'Athelstan King,
of earls the lord,
rewarder of heroes . . .'

More prosaic, but hardly less significant for posterity, was the activity of administration at Athelstan's court, where a steady flow of charters and technical, legal documents bore witness to the increasing sophistication of the Saxon state. Athelstan also went to great lengths to develop contacts with foreign

rulers. The Emperor Otto of Germany, Hugh Capet, Duke of the Franks, and Conrad, Duke of Burgundy, all married sisters of Athelstan, and Louis d'Outremer, King of the Franks, was brought up at Athelstan's court. Such connections were often begun, and then later cemented, by exchanges of gifts. In this the Saxon King excelled, both as a passionate collector and also as an open-handed dispenser of jewels, gold and silverwork, carvings and precious things of all sorts – and above all, sacred relics.

Of all the Saxon kings, Athelstan was the most magnificent. It is entirely fitting that he should be the first king of England to be depicted, on some of his coins, and in an illuminated manuscript, wearing what we have come to regard as an essential symbol of royalty – a gold crown.

King Athelstan, 'King of All Britain', presenting a copy of Bede's works to St Cuthbert.

Edmund   939–946

Born c.922
Crowned Kingston-upon-Thames
Buried Glastonbury

Edmund was barely eighteen when he succeeded his older brother on the throne, and his short reign made little mark on the chronicles. He was described as a 'protector of friends', and won high praise for the firmness with which he put down rebellions by the Mercian Danes and brought the Five Towns of the Danelaw (Derby, Leicester, Lincoln, Nottingham and Stamford) back to obedience. But his promising career ended abruptly and violently at a feast in his own hall. An outlaw, named Leof, insolently intruded among the guests, and drew his dagger when the major-domo tried to expel him. The King unwisely intervened, and was himself fatally stabbed. (Leof was instantly 'cut to pieces'.)

Edred   946–955

Born 925
Crowned Kingston-upon-Thames
Buried Winchester

At Edmund's sudden death, the crown passed once again to a brother, this time the 22-year-old Edred. Like his predecessor, he had to deal with trouble from the northern Danes, and put it down with what appears to have been a mixture of strength and subtlety, setting rival warlords against each other until the time was ripe (in 954) to take the whole northern kingdom back into direct Saxon control. Edred's vigour was all the more remarkable because he appears to have been physically weak, almost an invalid, with a problematic digestion which made him unable to stomach flesh – a serious social disadvantage in a carnivorous era. He died at Frome, of illness.

Eadwig   955–959

Born c.942
Crowned Kingston-upon-Thames
Died Gloucester

All the sons of Edward the Elder having reigned in turn, the Crown now passed to the next generation, the sons of Edmund. Eadwig (Edwy) was no more than thirteen when he succeeded, and his court was immediately beset with factions, the two most important of which focused on rival groups of royal ladies. Eadwig, who is described as having been singularly handsome, became entangled with one of these groups – but the other party included a number of powerful earls and bishops. Rebellion followed, Mercia and Northumbria broke away, and Eadwig died before he was twenty, leaving his enemies to write the history of the struggle, a task which they seem to have set about with positively suspicious relish. In other words, we find plenty of scandalous allegations, but very few reliable facts, in the chronicles of this reign.

Edgar's coronation, performed by Dunstan, Archbishop of Canterbury. A detail from The Edgar Window *in Bath Abbey.*

Edgar   959–975

Born 945
Crowned Bath
Buried Glastonbury

Edgar was aged only twelve when he was made ruler of Mercia and Northumbria, and fourteen when his brother's death made him King of Wessex as well. To begin with he must have been very much a figurehead rather than a leader, and some historians have been inclined to see his great reputation as the product of propaganda, particularly on the part of the Church. It seems unnecessary to go to such lengths of scepticism. Edgar's reign was conspicuously peaceful, and even if much of the credit for this state of affairs can go to the great noblemen and prelates who clustered round the King, they were unquestionably his men, and he both supported their work and held them in check.

In 973, curiously late in his reign, Edgar was solemnly anointed and crowned King, with ceremonies of great splendour and stateliness which seem to have provided the model for all later coronations. Later in the year, Edgar was met at Chester by a number of vassal kings from

Scotland and Wales, who rowed him in state along the River Dee. Not for nothing was he known as 'Edgar the glorious, by the grace of Christ illustrious King of the English and of the other people dwelling within the bounds of the island of Britain'.

One of the most notable achievements of Edgar's reign was a sweeping reform of the monasteries, carried out by three of the greatest figures in the history of the English Church, Dunstan of Canterbury, Oswald of York, and Ethelwold of Abingdon. The success of the reformers marked an important step in the development of the English state. At the same time it laid the foundation for future trouble, by encouraging the belief that the King could and should act as Christ's vicar on earth, towards the Church as towards laymen.

Edward the Martyr   975–978

Born c.963
Crowned Kingston-upon-Thames
Buried Wareham
Re-buried Shaftesbury

Edgar's untimely death threw the kingdom into turmoil. His older son, Edward, only thirteen years old, had to encounter the violent hostility of his stepmother, Aelfthryth, and quickly succumbed. In March 978 he was assassinated at Corfe, where he had gone to visit Aelfthryth.

After his death, Edward became a symbol of innocence oppressed, in the eyes of those who had reason to be discontented with the regime of his successor. Miracles were attributed to his relics, and he was elevated to sainthood.

Ethelred Unraed   978–1016

Born 968
Crowned Kingston-upon-Thames
Buried St Paul's

The name Ethelred is a compound of two old English words meaning 'noble counsel': 'Unraed' means 'no counsel' – or, alternatively, 'evil counsel' and 'treacherous plot'. We need look no further than the circumstances of Ethelred's accession to the throne, and the influence of his sinister mother Aelfthryth, to see the origins of his punning nickname. His subsequent failures

A coin depicting Ethelred, known as 'The Unready'. He fled to Normandy following the invasion by King Swein of Denmark.

against the Danes merely reinforced his reputation, though they were such as to cause later generations to distort his 'Unraed' into 'Unready'.

Throughout his long and inglorious reign Ethelred had a knack of picking the worst of men as his counsellors and subordinates, at least if we are to trust the writer of the Anglo-Saxon Chronicle. The chronicle frequently seethes with fury at the incompetence, cowardice and treachery of Ethelred's advisors. The King, for his part, emerges as a man with the mind and morals of a gangster. Ethelred's first recorded independent action was to ravage the lands of his own subjects, and the sum of his ideas for combating the Viking invasions was either to buy them off or, as on St Brice's Day in 1002, to order the massacre of any Dane who was trusting enough to live peaceably in Ethelred's own dominions.

Some modern historians have tried to justify Ethelred by suggesting that the Danes came looking merely for loot, so that it was wisdom on his part to supply them with what they sought, while avoiding confrontation. But this is to ignore the hideous reality of the damage inflicted on England by successive and increasingly heavy Viking raids, especially in the period 991–1012. Still more, it is to disregard the fact that Ethelred, starting with every advantage that Alfred lacked, contrived in thirty years to lose all that Alfred had gained for Saxon England. He even gave way as king in 1013 to King Swein of Denmark, his greatest enemy, and retired to

Normandy. But Swein died in 1014, and Ethelred returned to burden the throne of England for a few more months until his death in 1016.

Edmund Ironside   1016

Born 993
Crowned St Paul's
Buried Glastonbury

Ethelred's older son, Edmund, who was 22 years old in 1016, seems to have despised his father, and it is likely that only Ethelred's death prevented the young firebrand from taking matters into his own hands. Once free to act, he embarked on a whirlwind of fierce and highly mobile fighting against the Danes, which threw them into unaccustomed disorder. Southern England was cleared of marauders in a matter of months but during the fifth and last great battle of the campaign, at Ashingdon, near Rochford in Essex, the Saxon revival was reversed with great slaughter – principally through the treachery of Ethelred's evil genius and advisor, Eadric, whom Edmund had not felt strong enough to discard.

Edmund died shortly afterwards, at Oxford, probably worn out by his exertions.

Cnut   1016–1035

Born c.995
Crowned St Paul's
Buried Winchester

The accession of Swein's son Cnut (Canute) was a triumph for the power principle. The House of Wessex was not extinct, but none of its members could offer a plausible prospect of effective kingship, and the Viking penetration of Saxon England was now so complete that the Saxon Witan as well as the Viking warhost looked to Cnut the Dane for leadership.

Cnut proved fully equal to dealing with his new acquisition. Malcontent or unreliable Saxon elements were ruthlessly destroyed – an ugly process of which the only satisfactory feature was the long-overdue termination of Eadric's career of treachery and shame. The kingdom was briskly divided into administrative territories, and a heavy tax was levied without

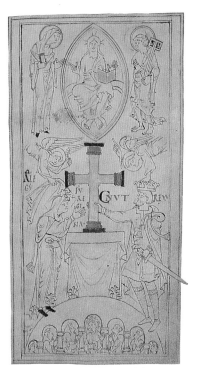

Cnut and Emma place a gold cross on the high altar of the New Minster at Winchester.

hesitation or compunction. Having made his mark, however, Cnut proceeded to show qualities of statesmanship as well as efficiency. He entrusted Saxons with the government of Saxons, paid off and dispersed his Danish army, and married Emma of Normandy, the widow of Ethelred. Then Cnut went on to codify and promulgate the customary laws, and ostentatiously identified himself as a pious son of the Church.

An exhausted England warmed to this treatment, and Cnut enjoyed the benefits of a solid power base when he embarked on a campaign of manoeuvres in Scandinavia in the 1020s. These made him the master of a mighty but short-lived Northern Empire, and one of the great powers of Europe.

King of Denmark and Norway, as well as of England, and acknowledged overlord of Scotland, the all-conquering Cnut was almost bound to receive flattery from his courtiers. In a famous episode, he rebuked their silly extravagance by forcing them to watch how the indifferent tide ignored the commands of the greatest of kings.

Coins depicting (ABOVE LEFT) *Harold I* and (ABOVE RIGHT) *Harthacnut. Harold's reign, like Harthacnut's, was brief and barbarous.*

Harold I   1035–1040

Born 1017
Crowned Oxford
Buried Westminster
Re-buried Southwark

When Cnut died at Shaftesbury, he intended his territories to be inherited, undivided, by Harthacnut, son of his second wife, Emma of Normandy. However, absence in Denmark worked against the designated heir, and Harold, older son by an earlier wife, won support for his claim to England. Harold's brief reign, like Harthacnut's in its turn, was a jackal-time in which packs of scavengers tore at the carcass of Cnut's empire, and savaged each other when they thought they were strong enough to escape retaliation. Harold is particularly remembered for his involvement in the treacherous blinding, and ultimate murder, of his half-brother Alfred at Guildford in 1036. He himself died at Oxford, aged 25.

Harthacnut   1040–1042

Born 1018
Crowned Canterbury
Buried Winchester

Harthacnut (Hardicanute) was on his way to invade England when his half-brother died, and throughout his short reign he treated the country as conquered territory, ruling with brutal greediness. He died drinking at a marriage feast, where 'he fell to the earth in a horrid convulsion'.

BELOW: *Edward the Confessor seated at a banquet.* RIGHT: *Harold swearing allegiance to William at Bayeux.* OPPOSITE BELOW: *The Norman Kings of England – William I, William II, Henry I and Stephen – represented as patrons of the Church. Each is holding a model of a church he founded.*

Edward the Confessor   1042–1066

Born 1004
Crowned Winchester
Buried Westminster

England's connection with Denmark died with Harthacnut, and the House of Wessex returned to the throne in the person of Edward, last surviving son of Ethelred Unraed. This new king had little in common with his Saxon ancestors. Half Norman by birth, he had spent most of his life until now in Normandy, and made little secret of his lasting preference for all things, and people, Norman. Although personally dignified, and even impressive, he was temperamentally torpid, and fell a ready prey to forceful and unscrupulous schemers, most prominent of whom was Godwin, the powerful Earl of Wessex. He was no warrior, and uninterested in the practicalities of government. His chief delights were hunting, religious observance and ecclesiastical aesthetics – hence his interest in the re-building of Westminster Abbey, which was consecrated in 1065. An accumulation of legends has emphasised Edward's piety, and he was declared a saint in 1161, but contemporary accounts tend to present him as an amiable dilettante.

Despite his weakness, Edward's reign was relatively peaceful. There was some vicious feuding among and within the great noble families, and a series of savage clashes with the Welsh. But the extreme urgencies of Ethelred's reign seemed to be things of the past, now that the Viking marauders had settled and become possessors of lands. The conflicts of the coming epoch were to be dynastic rather than tribal. Perhaps the worst that can be said against Edward the Confessor is that he failed to provide an heir to his throne, and left England open to aggression from the domesticated Vikings of Normandy.

Harold II　　　　　　　　　1066

Born 1022
Crowned Westminster
Buried near Hastings
Re-buried Waltham Abbey

Harold was the second son of Earl Godwin and had been supreme in the councils of King Edward since Godwin's death in 1053. In the absence of any close blood relative, Harold was the obvious choice as Edward's successor by the conventions of the time. He appears to have been designated so by the King on his deathbed before being elected by the Witanagemot and duly crowned and anointed.

Everything in Harold's career suggests that he would have made a ruler in the best Saxon tradition – brave, vigorous, honourable and generous. However, his position on the throne was challenged by two nearly simultaneous invasions. Although Harold destroyed the first of them, mounted in the north by his own brother Tostig and King Harald Hardrada of Norway, he over-extended his resources in trying to deal equally quickly with the second group of marauders, led against the south of England by William of Normandy. The first of his two battles, at Stamford Bridge near York, was a victory greater in scale than any won by Alfred or Athelstan; yet the second, at Hastings, was a defeat so conclusive that it totally overshadowed what had gone before. Harold was killed, either by an axe or an arrow, and his weakened forces were routed. Thereafter, Saxon England disintegrated.

William I
(the Conqueror)　　　1066–1087

Born 1028
Crowned Westminster
Buried Caen

William the Conqueror was descended from Viking freebooters and warlords who, from the middle of the ninth century, first plundered and then settled north-western France. He inherited his Duchy when only a boy, and the desperate struggle for survival that preoccupied his early years probably reinforced his natural tendency towards ruthlessness and resolution. He was a hard man in every sense – a ferocious warrior, a harsh ruler, a driving administrator and a man of vigorous principles. His willpower was massive and his temper was fearsome.

He claimed the English throne both on the grounds of a supposed act of 'designation' on the part of Edward, while the latter was in his long Norman exile, and of a shadowy promise extorted from Godwin's son Harold in 1064. In reality,

it was force of arms that mattered, and remarkably good luck. The invasion of 1066 was a gigantic gamble, and William swept the board.

Saxon resistance flared and spluttered for some years after Hastings, but William put down all outbreaks with relentless severity. The Saxon nobility were largely destroyed and almost totally dispossessed, in favour of Norman knights, and a similar process was applied to the Church. Unlike Cnut, who ruled England as he found it, William set his grip on England and changed it to suit his needs. The common people were still able to invoke the customary laws, but in great matters such as land tenure, taxation and military organisation the Normans developed a system of their own. It was one which in some ways went beyond what was to be found in Normandy itself. The great and meticulous Domesday survey of 1085 was both an expression of this system and its most astonishing achievement; nothing could give us a more telling insight into the personality of the King who caused it to be made.

William II (Rufus)   1087–1100

Born 1056
Crowned Westminster
Buried Winchester
William I left three sons to dispute his inheritance. The middle one, also called William, was first to reach England. He had himself swiftly crowned and seized the royal treasure with a promptness worthy of his father. William Rufus (from the redness of his face) was a professional soldier of his time – ruthless to the point of cruelty, recklessly greedy, cynically jovial and much admired by his knights. He cared not a rap for religion and behaved shockingly towards the Church; in this he was unwise, for the clergy wrote the chronicles. However, he kept the peace and suppressed two rebellions with success.

William Rufus was killed by an arrow, in 1100, while hunting in the New Forest. The circumstances of his death were odd, but contemporary accounts regarded it as an accident. Later historians with a taste for melodrama suggested murder and, most recently, black magic.

Silver penny of Henry I.

Henry I   1100–1135

Born 1070
Crowned Westminster
Buried Reading
Rufus' younger brother Henry was a member of the fatal hunting party in the New Forest, and hardly waited to see the body picked from the ground before galloping to nearby Winchester and seizing the royal treasury. Subsequently, he was lavish in his treatment of the family of the man who admitted firing the fatal shot. Throughout his career, Henry repeatedly showed a capacity for swift and violent action. He caused two of his own grand-daughters to be blinded in retaliation for their father's treatment of hostages and, in 1124–5, he had all the moneyers in England mutilated without trial, to discourage their successors from falsifying the coinage. He seems to have been naturally both cruel and avaricious. All the same, this heavy hand checked lawlessness in all parts of his kingdom, and although a much more calculating character than Rufus, he had the knack of winning admiration and even trust.

Henry reigned for the most part in peace. In 1106, however, he defeated his older brother Robert of Normandy in an unexpectedly decisive battle at Tinchebrai, seized his Duchy and imprisoned him for the rest of Robert's life.

One of Henry's first acts as King was to marry a descendant of Alfred the Great, a match with obvious dynastic overtones. Of his three legitimate children, one died in infancy, another – William – was drowned at sea and the third was a

daughter, Matilda, whom Henry married to the German Emperor Henry V. He therefore left a confused and problematic succession at his death in 1135.

Stephen   1135–1154

Born 1104
Crowned Westminster
Buried Faversham
Henry I attempted to bind his barons to accepting his daughter Matilda as his heiress, but in December 1135 it was Henry's much-loved nephew, Count Stephen of Blois, who was acclaimed and crowned King. Stephen is a fascinating character. His charm, geniality, dash and bravery made him almost universally popular, but he was also peculiarly unsuccessful in sustaining action of almost any sort, and repeatedly showed a streak of tricky unreliability.

He is best summed up in a story told by the chronicler William of Malmesbury, who relates how Stephen laid an ambush for the Earl of Gloucester, failed in the attempt and then tried to laugh it off 'by a genial countenance and an unsolicited confession'.

Stephen's rule was promptly challenged by Matilda, 'the Empress', as she was still commonly known, although her first husband had died in 1125; she had been remarried in 1128 to Count Geoffrey of Anjou. Matilda commanded enough support and enjoyed sufficient resources to throw Stephen's kingdom into turmoil. But neither party could muster the strength for a decisive blow. In 1141 Stephen was captured at Lincoln, but his Queen (also, confusingly, called Matilda) succeeded in a lucky counterstroke which brought about his release, and in 1142 the Empress was forced to make a dramatic escape through the snow from Oxford. When the Empress retired from active campaigning, her son Henry took up the struggle. For much of Stephen's reign, but especially between 1139 and 1145, there was anarchy in England. When Stephen's son Eustace died before his father, it was probably a relief for all concerned that the succession should be firmly settled on the young Henry.

Henry II   1154–1189

Born 1133
Crowned Westminster
Buried Fontevraud

Henry II has been described as 'one of the most remarkable characters in English history'. He ruled an empire greater than that of any English king before him – England, Wales, Ireland, Normandy, Anjou, Brittany and Aquitaine. Far more significant than this, he overwhelmed his contemporaries with the sheer force and brilliance of his temperament and talents. He was a figure of European stature, comparable in prestige to the Emperor Frederick Barbarossa. His wife, Eleanor of Aquitaine, was one of the most powerful and dynamic women of all medieval Europe. Their children and grandchildren became kings and queens of most countries between England and the Holy Land. Henry was a man of splendid physique, who was ceaselessly active and dazzlingly

versatile. He loved war, hunting, law, letters, art and architecture. His rages terrified people, his impetuosity exasperated them, his charm bewitched them. The explosive force of his will both awed his subjects and compelled them to follow him.

The most significant and lasting of Henry's works was his reconstruction of the English legal system. Laws and law courts, policing and legal procedures, all took strides forward under his fierce urging, and government became concerned, far more than ever before, with maintaining good order throughout the realm.

It was Henry's quarrels which impressed contemporaries more than his keeping of the peace. The most famous quarrel of all was that with his Chancellor, Thomas Becket. At its simplest it was a clash of two indomitable wills, who were too close to each other to live comfortably together. But there were also great issues of principle at stake in the conflict between the rights of the Church and the powers of the State. Henry had Becket murdered in his own cathedral in 1170. Later came quarrels with Queen Eleanor, and with his own sons, so that Henry's last days were spent in vicious civil war which threatened to bring the whole of his vast empire down in ruins. Only his own death frustrated the collapse.

Richard I
(Coeur de Lion)   1189–1199

Born 1157
Crowned Westminster
Buried Fontevraud

'Few English kings', writes Christopher Brooke, 'have played so small a part in the affairs of England and so large a part in the affairs of Europe as Richard I.' Richard was the complete cosmopolitan military adventurer – tough, glamorous, a brilliant general and a restless wanderer. As a king of England he was a disaster. He spent only two short spells in the country, one of three months and one of two; otherwise, he was campaigning in France, Sicily and Palestine, where in 1191 he fought his way to within twelve miles of Jerusalem. England paid for his exploits and paid again in 1192, when he was captured at Vienna on his way back from the Crusade. He died of a wound, sustained largely through carelessness, in 1199. He was a homosexual and left no son.

John   1199–1216

Born 1167
Crowned Westminster
Buried Worcester

It fell to Richard's only surviving brother, John, to meet the series of internal upheavals and external assaults which, almost inevitably, assailed the unmanageably vast

ABOVE: *Henry II enthroned, a nineteenth-century engraving.* RIGHT: *The coronation procession of Richard I approaching Westminster in 1189, from a Flemish manuscript.*

11

empire of Henry II. He faced these challenges with indomitable vigour and much ability, but fought a losing battle and died in the shadow of failure.

In John's attempt to maintain his position, he rode roughshod over the Church and many of the nobility. His clash with the clergy caused England to be placed under Papal interdict between 1208 and 1214, and involved John in excommunication from 1209 to 1213. Subsequently, however, the Pope became John's closest ally. A rebellious faction of the nobility forced John in 1215 to concede at Runnymede, near Windsor, a list of privileges which has achieved almost legendary status as Magna Carta. 'The cornerstone of English liberties,' was how subsequent generations came to see it, though the fact of the King's being forced to make concessions was more important than the concessions themselves.

John's reputation has been radically affected by the outcome of these quarrels, and he has received less than his due for his abilities as a brilliant commander in land warfare, an imaginative pioneer of naval defence and an inventive and energetic administrator.

John's greatest problem was the disloyalty of his barons. The lords of John's French lands were bound to develop French rather than English allegiances, and it can be argued that in losing Normandy John clarified the future for the kingdom of England.

Henry III   1216–1272

Born 1207
Crowned Gloucester
Buried Westminster

The reign of Henry III saw constitutional developments of the utmost importance. These came about more because of the weaknesses of the King than because of his strengths. Throughout his reign, noble factions struggled for control over the crown. Under the pressure of their rivalries, the concept of absolute royal power was modified to accommodate the principle of consultation.

The basic strength of the monarchy was shown by the speed with which it shook off the chaos that closed over John at the end. However, the advisers who had managed the young King's affairs so successfully before he took matters into his own hands in 1227, soon found that it was a different matter to be servants. The years of Henry's personal rule until 1258 were marked by a series of minor crises in which the baronage tried to strengthen their position, often on the basis laid by Magna Carta. For his part, Henry showed a preference for foreign advisers and a taste for European power play, which split the Court into factions. The Angevin Empire was formally buried by agreement with Louis IX of France in 1259, leaving only Gascony in English hands, but by then the discontent of the barons had boiled over.

In 1258 Henry was forced to accept a settlement known as the Provisions of Oxford, which effectively established a baronial council to regulate the King's government. The leader of the barons was a Frenchman, Simon de Montfort, who combined great personal force and practical effectiveness with a far-ranging vision and grasp of political trends. Henry not unnaturally struggled against the constraints with which de Montfort and his friends sought to bind him, and

ABOVE: *King John portrayed hunting. In 1215 the barons forced him to seal the Magna Carta, which has become 'the cornerstone of English liberties'.* BELOW: *Henry III, a detail from the effigy on his tomb in Westminster Abbey.*

civil war broke out in 1264. The King lost the first round at the battle of Lewes, and de Montfort attempted to consolidate the government with the help of a specially summoned 'Great Council', including representatives of the shires and the towns of England – a gathering which is regarded as the forerunner of modern parliaments. In 1265, however, Henry's son Edward turned the tables, at Evesham, where the barons were defeated and de Montfort was killed.

Henry had an exalted view of his royal status while lacking the force and talents to make good his claims. He loved splendour and display, but lacked judgement and asserted himself more obstinately than shrewdly. He greatly admired Edward the Confessor, whom he somewhat resembled. He was conspicuously pious, rebuilt Westminster Abbey and named his only son Edward.

Edward I   1272–1307

Born 1239
Crowned Westminster
Buried Westminster

Edward I might be taken as a pattern of the medieval king. He is remembered on the whole for his achievements rather than by his personality.

Tall, strong and handsome in figure, he was magnificently royal in presence, clear and emphatic in speech, forceful and enterprising in action. He was uncertain in temper, but reasonable in council. Above all, he attempted to live by the ideal of Christian knighthood – devoutly gallant and heroically chivalrous. There was little of the fanatic in Edward: he was a pragmatic Englishman, who was formidable under stress and disliked muddle at all times, but who was happiest on horseback with his dogs at his heels and a hawk on his wrist.

The turbulent princes of Wales, under their new leader Llywylyn, were defeated and brought to order in the first ten years of Edward's reign. By the Statute of Wales (1284) the principality was finally annexed to the English crown. As a gesture of reconciliation, the King's new-born son was proclaimed Prince of Wales at Caernarvon Castle, and the title

has been held by successive heirs to the throne ever since.

Edward's attempt to assert his overlordship of the Scots was complicated elsewhere by French attacks on his Gascon possessions. Although he secured considerable success in Scotland in 1296 and again in 1298, when he defeated Wallace at Falkirk and carried off the Scottish coronation stone of Scone, Scottish resistance continued under the leadership of Robert Bruce. 'The hammer of the Scots', as Edward had become known, died in 1307 as he moved north on yet another campaign.

Apart from his achievements in strengthening the unity of what became Great Britain, Edward was a powerful and effective law-giver. He was also a formidable administrator, a great builder and a statesman of European reputation. It is hardly surprising that in later years his reign came to take on almost the quality of a golden age.

Edward II   1307–1327

Born 1285
Crowned Westminster
Buried Gloucester

The military triumphs of Edward I had been bought at a heavy cost in taxes, and a new generation of baronial opposition had begun to

TOP: *Edward I in Parliament, flanked by the King of Scotland and the Prince of Wales.* ABOVE: *Effigy of Edward II in Gloucester Cathedral. Pilgrims flocked to the tomb of the late King, revering him as a saint.*

make itself felt towards the end of his reign. When, under the new king, victory in war was replaced by defeat, discontent rose and the years of Edward II's reign were marked by civil war and political confusion.

Edward's ineptitude as a soldier was demonstrated at Bannockburn, in 1314, when Robert Bruce destroyed the English army with humiliating completeness. This battle assured Scottish independence for a further three centuries and condemned northern England to be a barren borderland ruled by war lords. It also precipitated trouble in every other part of the kingdom. Edward's frivolous, lazy and extravagant behaviour did much to alienate his barons (the chronicles speak of his 'wonted fatuity'). His addiction to favourites, especially to Piers Gaveston and Hugh Despenser, was a more damaging weakness. Baronial opposition intensified, and from 1322 there was open civil war.

Events in Gascony repeated and heightened the Scottish story. The French King seized Edward's possessions and provided a spark that exploded the situation in England. Eventually it was Isabella, Edward's own Queen and the sister of Charles IV of France, in combination with a faction of the nobility, that brought about his fall. He was deposed in 1327 and murdered in Berkeley Castle later the same year.

Edward III presides over a jousting tournament.

Edward III   1327–1377

Born 1312
Crowned Westminster
Buried Westminster

'The English', wrote the Chronicler Froissart, 'will never love and honour a king unless he be victorious and a lover of arms and war.' Like his grandfather, Edward III gave his people the triumphs they wanted. But he, too, outlived his success.

In his early years, Edward was used as a pawn by his mother and her lover, Roger Mortimer. In 1330, however, the young Prince asserted himself, executed Mortimer and ordered his mother into retirement. Internal feuding was put aside and a national effort was directed towards external enemies, especially the French, who were threatening the English possessions in Aquitaine, and the Scots, who represented a menace to the north.

The military and political efforts required to wage the vast campaigns which brought Edward his fame led to developments of lasting significance in the fields of state administration and the relationship between Crown and Parliament (which granted the essential taxes). Edward III was less of a law-giver than his grandfather, but his achievements make him no less important as a builder of the English state.

Edward won sea battles against France at Sluys (1340), and Castile off Winchelsea (1350). He defeated the Scots at Halidon Hill (1333), and his army beat them again even more decisively at Neville's Cross (1345) while he was himself in France. He wrote the names of two of the greatest of English battle honours at Crécy (1346) and Poitiers (1356). The King of Scotland was captured at Neville's Cross, the King of France at Poitiers; and Edward shone forth as the greatest warrior of western Europe. It was while he was at the peak of his career as a leader of chivalry that he founded the Order of the Knights of the Garter in 1348.

The second half of the reign was a sadder story. The plague of the Black Death struck England in 1348–9, killing roughly one-third of the population within 10 years, and radically altering society. At the same time the tide of war turned against English arms, both at sea and on land. And Edward himself lapsed into a slack and ineffectual dotage, in which he was incapable of resisting the turbulence of his Parliament. He was old, for a medieval king, but it was a sad and degrading end.

Richard II   1377–1399

Born 1367
Crowned Westminster
Buried Langley
Re-buried Westminster

Edward the Black Prince, the famous son of Edward III, died before his father, and it was a child of ten who succeeded to the throne in 1377. Richard's reign began in a confusion that deepened into crisis. After a central period of relative calm, events slid again into civil war. The King's personality had much to do with his difficulties, at least at the latter end. But European society itself was diseased in this period of the Black Death, as the Speaker of the House of Commons recognised when in 1381 he voiced the fear that 'the whole kingdom will be lost and utterly destroyed for ever, and our lord the King and the Lords and Commons along with it.'

The first great crisis of the reign was the Peasants' Revolt in 1381. It was an episode that looked back to innumerable riots of the desperate and starving, but also forward to modern political revolutions. The boy King showed extraordinary bravery and self-control in calming the mob in a moment of the most intense danger at Smithfield, and their threat receded. The aristocracy

LEFT: *Richard II enthroned. Richard, the son of the Black Prince, was crowned aged ten.* BELOW: *The effigy of Henry IV, first sovereign of the House of Lancaster, on his tomb in Canterbury Cathedral.*

Henry of Bolingbroke, the Duke of Lancaster. He resigned the Crown in September 1399, and was probably murdered at Pontefract Castle early in 1400.

In its heyday, Richard's court was one of the most splendid and sophisticated in Europe. He was the patron of Chaucer and of the painter of the Wilton Diptych. He was brilliant and inventive, and if his bid for absolutism had succeeded he might now be remembered as the founder of a despotism to rival those of contemporary France and Italy. But after his bravery as a boy at Smithfield, he never again carried his people with him.

Henry IV	1399–1413

Born 1367
Crowned Westminster
Buried Canterbury

Henry of Bolingbroke's claim to the throne was debatable. It rested more on the impossibility of continuing with Richard II than on any consideration of right. Hopes expressed at his accession for a time of order and the rule of law were to be disappointed. The years to 1405 were plagued by uprisings, particularly in Wales and the north. And although all in turn were defeated,

were as disordered as the peasantry, and the later 1380s saw a round of bitter fighting which was checked only when Richard seized power for himself in 1389.

For several years there was something approaching calm; but in 1397 Richard seems to have decided to try to achieve complete authority, amounting to royal absolutism, by the use of arbitrary violence, intimidation and terror. Richard overreached himself, lost support and was forced to submit to his cousin,

15

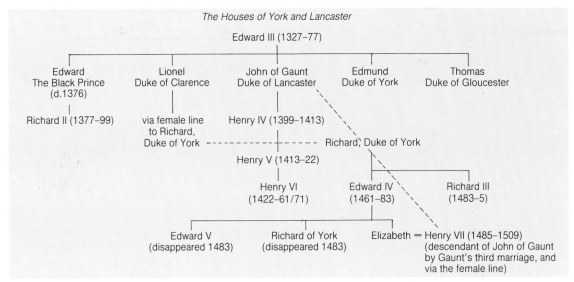

The Houses of York and Lancaster

Edward III (1327–77)

Edward
The Black Prince
(d.1376)

Lionel
Duke of Clarence

John of Gaunt
Duke of Lancaster

Edmund
Duke of York

Thomas
Duke of Gloucester

Richard II (1377–99)

via female line
to Richard,
Duke of York

Henry IV (1399–1413)

Richard, Duke of York

Henry V (1413–22)

Henry VI
(1422–61/71)

Edward IV
(1461–83)

Richard III
(1483–5)

Edward V
(disappeared 1483)

Richard of York
(disappeared 1483)

Elizabeth = Henry VII (1485–1509)
(descendant of John of Gaunt
by Gaunt's third marriage, and
via the female line)

they created a turbulence which persisted long after the great battles such as Shrewsbury (1403) had been lost and won. Indeed, the names of the leading rebels, Owen Glyndowr and Henry Percy (Harry Hotspur), have passed, with Shakespeare's help, into popular imagination.

Henry was beset by financial difficulties. His frequent demands that Parliament should give help in the form of taxes opened the door to long discussions about grievances, which sometimes led to intense wranglings, full of significance for the future of the constitution.

Henry himself was a tough warrior, and a shrewd manager of men but, as Maurice Keen remarks, 'no-one regretted his days when they were over'. When contrasted with the courtly splendours of his cousin Richard II, or the military glories of his son Henry V, his reign lacks ambition and achievement.

Henry V   1413–1422

Born 1387
Crowned Westminster
Buried Westminster

Henry V is unrivalled among the late medieval kings of England, for both success and sheer ability. This was a distinction made all the more impressive by the fact that his riotous youth meant that all the achievements were crowded into the nine years of his short reign. He embodied so completely the ideal qualities of medieval kingship that it is tempting to describe him as a

symbol of the entire era – the more so that this finest flower of knighthood was practically the last of his line. Henry's devotion to chivalrous combat, his orthodox piety, even his concept of kingly justice, were about to be superseded by the warfare of gunpowder, the reformation of religion and the statecraft of the Renaissance.

The central fact of Henry's reign was the conquest of France. The internal troubles of the French kingdom gave Henry a chance to reassert claims inherited from the Plantagenets. In two great expeditions (1415 and 1417–18) England's continental empire was briefly restored. At Agincourt, in October 1415, the French chivalry were mown down in swathes by English archers as the French attempted to sweep over Henry's trapped and outnumbered forces. In the later expedition, a campaign of ruthlessly organised sieges subdued the cities of Normandy and returned that Duchy to the English crown.

The climax of Henry's success was reached with the Treaty of Troyes in 1420. By this treaty he took as wife Catherine of Valois, daughter of the French King, Charles VI, and was assured of the reversion of the French throne to England after Charles' death. Fortune, however, prevented it. Henry V died of dysentery on his third campaigning expedition in 1422, and was just outlived by the feeble Charles VI of France. Henry's son proved to be as weak as his father had been strong.

Henry VI   1422–1461/1470–71

Born 1421
Crowned Westminster
Buried Chertsey
Re-buried Windsor

The long reign of Henry VI was as disastrous as the short reign of his father had been glorious. The regencies of his childhood, although at first successful, established a pattern of ambition among the nobility which ran out of control as time went by. Henry was a man of weak will, no better than simple-minded in the eyes of his enemies. He was out of his depth in the vicious intrigues of his Court, under the pressures of which he suffered periodic bouts of nervous collapse. He was also a visionary, one for whom the Song of the Angels was more than a mere figure of speech. His preoccupations were with scholarship, music, architecture, the worship of God and the creation of ordered communities in which men could follow regular lives devoted to the pursuit of truth and beauty. So he founded Eton and King's College, Cambridge, lost all his father's conquests in France, and failed to stop England sliding into the terrible convulsions of the Wars of the Roses.

The King's feebleness, though central, was not the whole of the story. The French, formerly demoralised, were rallied by Joan of Arc in 1429, and the diplomacy of the continental war was radically altered by a change of alliances in

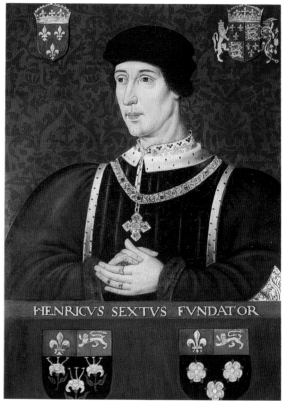

HENRICVS SEXTVS FVNDATOR

1435. At home, the decay of feudalism, that filled England with armed men bearing the badges of rival lords, posed problems of enormous size and complexity.

Whatever the causes of the débacle, Normandy was finally lost in 1450 and Gascony in 1451. The civil war in England between the followers of Richard, Duke of York, a descendant of Edward III, and the royal (or Lancastrian) party dominated by Henry's formidable wife Margaret of Anjou, swayed to and fro from the early 1450s. Henry himself was more victim than actor in all this: mad, imprisoned, deposed and restored, he was a mere pawn in the game. Henry was murdered in the Tower in 1471.

Edward IV   1461–70/1471–83

Born 1441
Crowned Westminster
Buried Windsor

Richard, Duke of York, whose bid for power in 1455 precipitated the Wars of the Roses, was killed in 1460. His son, Edward, reversed the verdict of battle in 1461, at Towton in Yorkshire, and made good his claim to the throne. Dashing and active, he had great talents as a soldier, an administrator and a philanderer, though time was to show him unreliable and vengeful in addition. He came through a crisis between 1469 and 1471, when his former ally, the Earl of Warwick (the King Maker), tried to achieve supremacy by switching to the Lancastrian side, thus bringing about the temporary restoration of Henry VI. But Warwick was destroyed at the Battle of Barnet, and King Henry's son Edward was killed at the Battle of Tewkesbury three weeks later — which opened the way for the murder of the father in turn. Edward's position was secure, if not exactly untroubled, when he died suddenly in 1483.

He had been secretly married to Elizabeth Woodville, and this marriage, together with the inevitable advancement of the fortunes of the Woodville family, was deeply resented, and after the King's death the marriage was declared invalid. Henry VII, however, later restored Elizabeth as Queen Dowager. She refounded Queens' College, Cambridge, and died in 1492.

ABOVE LEFT: *Henry V, the warrior king who won a great victory over the French at Agincourt in 1415.*
ABOVE RIGHT: *Henry VI, who founded Eton and King's College, Cambridge.*
BELOW: *Edward IV, who claimed the throne from the Lancastrians as the true heir of the deposed Richard II.*

Edward V   1483

Born 1470
Murdered in the Tower of London

Edward IV had nominated his brother, Richard of Gloucester, as protector of the realm in the event of his own early death. Edward could not have foreseen that Gloucester would stage a coup and take the throne for himself. With shocking suddenness, leading figures of the the old reign were swept up and executed, and the boy King, together with his brother Richard, Duke of York, disappeared into the Tower. There is no indisputable evidence that the two princes were murdered on the orders of Richard; but there is little doubt that this is what happened. What were thought to be their bones were uncovered in 1674; more likely remains came to light in the 1980s.

Edward V depicted with the crown placed over and above his head (in token that he was never crowned), from a fifteenth-century painted panel.

Richard III   1483–1485

Born 1452
Crowned Westminster
Buried Leicester

Few kings of England have attracted more controversy than Richard III. While some historians see him as a bloodstained monster, others regard him as tragically maligned and a few view him as the English prototype of a Renaissance ruler. Richard certainly had great abilities, as he had shown governing the north of England during his brother's reign. That he was ruthless in disposing of rivals there is no doubt, but it is hard to see anything really original in his approach to governing, and he failed to command the admiration of contemporaries as his brother Edward had done.

Richard weathered a revolt against his rule in late 1483, but a second attempt in 1485, led by Henry Tudor, Earl of Richmond, was successful. Richard fell fighting at Bosworth Field, in Leicestershire, where Lord Stanley picked Richard's crown from a hawthorn bush where it had fallen, and placed it on Henry Tudor's head.

Henry VII   1485–1509

Born 1457
Crowned Westminster
Buried Westminster

Henry Tudor's claim to the throne was flimsy. By virtue of his mother's descent from John of Gaunt he stood in the Lancastrian line but, like the Yorkists before him, he took the Crown of England by force of arms and held it by strength and skill. On both sides the leadership had been much reduced in numbers as a result of thirty years of battles, murders and executions, and Henry's judicious marriage with Elizabeth of York, daughter of Edward IV, began the process of binding together the great factions which had torn England apart since the death of Henry V.

Henry's government was prudent, managerial, efficient and unostentatious – as far removed in style from the military chivalry of Henry V as it was from the current Renaissance despotisms of Italy. Trouble, when it occurred, was put down firmly but without recourse to vengeful blood baths, and if Henry's foreign policy was studiedly unadventurous, it was also productive of considerable commercial benefit.

Henry VII was not a figure to attract popular affection; but he gave peace and security to England for twenty-four years.

Henry VIII   1509–1547

Born 1491
Crowned Westminster
Buried Windsor

The colourless astuteness of Henry VII contrasts strangely with the flamboyance and imperiousness of his son. Henry VIII stands out as a colossus among English kings. Gigantic in appetites, destructiveness and creativity, he slammed the door of history on the Middle Ages and thrust England into a new era.

In his youth Henry was a splendid figure, strong, skilled in every physical and artistic accomplishment, fearsome and generous. Henry flung away his father's carefully-hoarded treasure in wild pursuit of foreign adventures, that signified little and brought no reward. England alone had insufficient weight to stand up to the imperial super-states which emerged in Europe at the end of the fifteenth century. More money was soon needed and one of the great themes of the reign began to emerge, the King's willingness to take any action which would satisfy his need for cash.

A second motive, no less powerful, began to emerge in the late 1520s, the need for a male heir. And when his wife Catherine of Aragon, who was the widow of Henry's elder brother Arthur, failed to produce a living son, Henry convinced himself that this must be because the marriage was invalid in the eyes of God. An annulment could only come from the Pope – but the Pope was under the influence of Catherine's nephew, the King of Spain. So began a conflict with Rome which led to the dissolution of the monasteries (1536–9) and the establishment of a national State Church. No single episode is more important in the whole of English history. Almost at a blow, Henry shattered the whole medieval ecclesiastical culture, and prepared the way for renewed religious, social and economic activity.

ABOVE LEFT: *Richard III, who met his death on Bosworth Field in battle with the Lancastrians.* ABOVE RIGHT: *Henry VII. His victory over Richard made him king and founder of the Tudor dynasty.* RIGHT: *The boy king Edward VI who bears a striking resemblance to his grandfather Henry (above).*

After Catherine of Aragon, Henry married five more times. His last wife outlived him, but by then two had been divorced, one had died in childbirth, and two more were executed.

Edward VI	1547–1553

Born 1537
Crowned Westminster
Buried Westminster

After bringing so many convulsions upon England in his search for a male heir, Henry VIII died leaving only one son, a sickly child of ten. Edward VI was an intelligent, perhaps even promising child but could be no more than a pawn in the hands of the magnates who now threatened, briefly, to bring back the

anarchy of the Wars of the Roses. The King's uncle, the Earl of Hertford (later Duke of Somerset) held power as Protector until his fall and execution in 1552, when he was succeeded by the Earl of Warwick (later Duke of Northumberland). The regimes of both men favoured the 'new' religious ideas that Henry VIII had kept at bay, and thus the short reign of Edward VI saw the Reformation converted into a Protestant phenomenon. The young King, who was priggish as well as precocious, appears to have approved.

Edward died of consumption, or perhaps of over-medication.

Mary I   1553–1558

Born 1516
Crowned Westminster
Buried Westminster

Mary was the daughter of Henry VIII and Catherine of Aragon. She was declared a bastard when Henry repudiated her mother, and during Edward's reign came under pressure to conform to the Protestant faith. It is perhaps not surprising that when she came to the throne she devoted herself to the restoration of what she saw as the true religion.

Mary married King Philip of Spain in Winchester Cathedral in 1554. Her husband was entirely her choice, and her marriage provoked a rebellion among the newly Protestant gentry of Kent. The Protestant bishops Ridley and Latimer were burnt at the stake in 1555, and Archbishop Cranmer in 1556. They were among a total of some 300 Protestant victims. This, too, was Mary's policy, in outline if not entirely in detail, and it earned her the name 'Bloody Mary'.

Yet this stubborn woman presents a sad figure. Her Spanish husband despised her and left her. She never

conceived the child she so much longed for, and she began to realise that her persecutions were only completing the conversion of England to the Protestant religion. In the closing months of her reign the English lost Calais – last relic of a once-proud empire.

Elizabeth I   1558–1603

Born 1533
Crowned Westminster
Buried Westminster

When Henry VIII discarded Catherine of Aragon in favour of Anne Boleyn, it was partly because he saw a temper that matched his own. In Elizabeth, daughter of this second marriage, we see a mingling of traits from both parents: her father's strength, will, pride, ferocity and passion for splendour, and her mother's coquettishness, insincerity and magnetism. To her inheritance, she added a first-class mind, a rare capacity for judging men and events, a caution that trembled just this side of meanness and a pragmatic view of the world that put her not so much ahead of, but rather outside her own time.

Elizabeth I was the last great

monarch to rule as well as reign in England, and she presided over a nation that suddenly came into an accession of strength. The Queen can hardly be given credit for the achievements of Shakespeare and Spencer, Hilliard and Byrd, but she maintained a court within which their dazzling talents found employment and support. And certainly the more physical triumphs of Drake and Raleigh, Frobisher and Grenville owed everything to her policies at home and abroad.

The doubts and dangers of Elizabeth's early years did much to instil in her that ambiguity which so often exasperated her followers. When political considerations required clarity, however, she could be clear. She perceived straightaway that her role must be that of a Protestant sovereign and, whatever her private views, she proclaimed the patriotic necessity of Protestantism with unfailing vigour.

She was never without favourites, but she never let them take control of her will. Similarly, while she never ceased to be active abroad, she never committed herself to a leading role or an irreversible policy. Only once did her nerve falter, when she had to face the hideous necessity and the appalling precedent of executing a fellow sovereign, Mary, Queen of Scots.

The summit of Elizabeth's glory was reached in 1588, when the huge fleets of Spain were defeated by Lord Howard and blown away by winds. The destruction of the Spanish Armada occasioned a positive ecstasy of patriotic fervour in England, in all of which the almost divine figure of the Queen, Gloriana, occupied the central place. It was more than mere escapism that caused later generations to look back with wistful pride on 'the golden days of Good Queen Bess.'

James I   1603–1625

Born 1566
Crowned Westminster
Buried Westminster

Elizabeth's refusal to marry ensured the continuance of her own power so long as she lived, but also the extinction of her dynasty when she died. However, James VI of Scotland could claim the throne by virtue of descent, through his great-grandmother, the daughter of Henry VII. It was a curiously inadvertent way in which to end centuries of conflict between Scotland and England.

James was small, awkward and ungainly in person. He slobbered

ABOVE: *Charles I, who was brought to trial and executed in 1649. The King faced death with courage and dignity.*

BELOW LEFT: *James I, first Stuart king of England, who by his accession to the throne united the Kingdoms of England, Scotland and Ireland.*

OPPOSITE: *Charles II, who returned to the throne from his many years in exile vowing never again to 'go on his travels'.*

and spluttered and had a speech impediment. He was a bundle of phobias, and was afflicted with strong views on a wide range of matters, notably the evils of tobacco, witchcraft and puritanism. He was also much given to demonstrative homosexual behaviour. Unusually learned, he was fully convinced that he ruled by divine authority. All of these attributes, in their different ways, caused trouble for him in England. But by far the most serious difficulties focused on his relations with the Puritans and Parliament – complicated by the fact that the Puritans were increasingly strongly represented in Parliament. An inept administration and a foolishly spend-thrift foreign policy meant that James was always in

need of money, and his insensitive handling of religious issues guaranteed that Parliament would object to his requests for taxes. The stage was set for confrontation.

Charles I   1625–1649

Born 1600
Crowned Westminster
Buried Windsor

Charles I embodies a certain type of English king (others would be Henry III and Richard II) – cultured, autocratic and unwise. He was a great patron of the arts and a collector, and with his elegant and vivacious French Queen, Henrietta Maria, he established a style at his court which was sophisticated but sober.

Charles's inclinations in religion and government could be described as courtly. He favoured the restrained ceremonial and authoritative Church organisation of the Arminians, or High Church party, and disdained the undisciplined fanaticism of the Puritans. He turned away, as soon as he could, from the undignified business of haggling with Parliament over taxes, and sought to operate an efficient, centralised administration

paid for from sources within the royal prerogative. In Archbishop Laud and Thomas, Earl of Strafford, he found admirable and faithful servants to execute his policies. All went well so long as there was no need for emergency expenditure. When the Scots resisted attempts to modify their religious settlement, however, Parliament had to be summoned to vote funds and bitter confrontation followed. Religious and constitutional issues were mingled with economically based rivalries to produce an explosive mixture which erupted into civil war in 1642.

The Royalists fought bravely but not always shrewdly, and were eventually outmatched by the Parliamentary forces. The English Civil War was by no means a struggle of aristocrats against commoners. But it was the case that popular support was more effectively martialled by the Parliamentary leaders, most notable of whom was a country gentleman from Huntingdon, Oliver Cromwell.

It was the army rather than Parliament that won the war, and eventually arrested, tried and executed Charles in 1649. He was beheaded outside the magnificent banqueting house which he had ordered to be built in the latest style only a few years before. Politically, it was a totally unnecessary end, but he faced it with impeccable courage and 'nothing in his life became him like the leaving it.'

Charles II   1649–1685

Born 1630
Crowned Scone 1651 and
Westminster 1661
Buried Westminster

Kings are easier to destroy than to replace, as those who executed Charles I found to their confusion. A source of authority had gone, and neither Parliament nor army was quite clear how to make good the deficiency. While Oliver Cromwell lived his commanding personality held affairs together, but uncertainty prevailed after his death in 1658 until the army acted to bring back the monarchy, in the person of Charles II.

The restored King was able, charming, and inflexible on only

one point – his determination never again to 'go on his travels'. So, although he and his courtiers set out to enjoy themselves with a dissolute abandon far removed from the morality and restraint of his father's time, Charles II took care not to put himself into political danger at home. As it was, the commercial rivalry of Holland, and the looming power of France under Louis XIV, provided quite sufficient dangers from abroad. Two wars were fought against the Dutch, with varied success, and a rather devious policy of alliance with France was much disliked in England. These policies resulted in a steady growth of British naval power and commercial prosperity.

Charles was described by a contemporary as 'an exact knower of mankind', and in his cynical way he played his cards successfully right to the end.

James II   1685–1688 (deposed)

Born 1633
Crowned Westminster
Buried St Germain

James II was the younger son of Charles I. From an early age he proved brave and competent as a soldier and naval commander, and during the reign of Charles II he showed outstanding talent as administrator in charge of the great expansion of the Royal Navy. He was also serious-minded, humourless and stubborn – qualities which he inherited from his father. Unfortunately he completely lacked his brother's cynical sense of self-preservation.

When in 1672 he was converted by the example of his wife to Roman Catholicism, he provoked a storm which could have been avoided if he had chosen to do so. Repeated attempts were made to exclude him from the succession before Charles II died, but James ascended the throne in 1685 and promptly embarked upon a policy which was aimed at achieving arbitrary power for himself and the conversion of England to Roman Catholicism. The country would stand for neither of these, and in 1688 a formal invitation was sent to William, Prince of Orange, James's son-in-law (and nephew).

James II, a portrait painted during his exile in France.

The invasion which followed met practically no resistance. James fled to France, where he died in 1701.

William III and Mary II   1689–1694
William III (alone)   1694–1702

William III born 1650
Mary II born 1662
Both crowned Westminster
Both buried Westminster

When the outcome of the invasion of 1688 was confirmed by special Convention Parliaments in England and Scotland, it was more than a change of face under the Crown. The monarchy was now a Parliamentary institution, and kings and queens of Great Britain have reigned ever since in accordance with rules and conventions agreed with Parliament. The definition of the sovereign body is 'the King (or Queen) in Parliament'. Such a formula by no means reduces the monarchs to a position of insignificance; but it is a different situation from that occupied by William I or Henry VIII.

The new joint monarchs were unflamboyant figures. Mary was a gentle, unassertive creature, much given to good works and well liked. William was shrewd, tough and lacking in charm. The driving force of the reign was the need to create and maintain a coalition against the vast power of France (where James II had taken refuge). 'Dutch William's wars' were unpopular in England, but since they were fought by an army under the control of Parliament, the scope for complaint was limited. William continued to reign in his own right after Mary died of smallpox in 1694.

Anne   1702–1714

Born 1665
Crowned Westminster
Buried Westminster

William and Mary left no children and the throne passed to Mary's sister, Anne, a resolutely ordinary woman who was a devoted supporter of the Church of England and the Tory party. Regular party politics had begun to emerge with the formalisation of Parliamentary power in 1688. The Tories were the more monarchical group, the Whigs were inclined to emphasise the balancing role of the aristocracy.

Anne had few ideas but strong loyalties. For much of her reign, she was particularly devoted to her friend Sarah Jennings. Sarah was the wife of the first Duke of Marlborough, and the Duke's brilliant successes in the great wars with France (the battles of Blenheim, Oudenarde, Ramillies, Malplaquet) owed much to the support he received from home until his wife fell from favour in 1710.

Anne was married to Prince George of Denmark, an amiable, inconsequential man, with whom she had 17 children, all of whom died in infancy or early childhood. She was the last monarch to preside at a meeting of the Privy Council, and to refuse assent to a Parliamentary bill.

RIGHT: *Queen Anne, whose reign saw the union of England with Scotland, which previously had separate legislative procedures.* BELOW: *William III and his wife Mary II, who reigned as joint monarchs until Mary's death from smallpox, after which William ruled alone.*

George I 1714–1727

Born 1660
Crowned Westminster
Buried Hanover

George, Elector of Hanover, was only distantly related to the English Royal Family, but he was nonetheless the nearest Protestant heir, and the Act of Settlement of 1701 had stipulated that the throne could pass only to Protestants. He was wholly German in language, culture and political outlook, and found his English inheritance strange and uncongenial. His feelings were largely reciprocated by his new subjects, but since he had the good sense to leave the government entirely in the hands of English politicians, he experienced practically no active opposition, once a feeble pro-Stuart revolt had been put down in Scotland (1715). In fact, the accident of George's unalterable Germanness gave rise to a constitutional development of the first importance. Rather than attempt to deal with English politicians and Parliaments himself, the King formed the habit of entrusting his interests entirely to a chosen minister, who for his part had to be able to undertake to 'deliver' a favourable Parliamentary vote on the matter of the royal salary. Thus, in effect, began the office of Prime Minister.

George was a man of dogged temper, coarse sensibilities and set habits. He spent as much time as he could in Hanover, and died on his way there in 1727.

George II 1727–1760

Born 1683
Crowned Westminster
Buried Westminster

The second George was a man about whom there are plenty of anecdotes, but few weighty things to be said. He was a self-important, methodical, fussy, hard-working, petty-minded, skirt-chasing little man. He presided, without great enthusiasm, over a period of unprecedented prosperity for Britain at home and abroad. It was the heyday of the English aristocracy, whose great and beautiful houses studded the land. The royal court, by contrast, was a dull and almost insipid affair, redeemed only by the King's passion for music, and admiration for Handel.

George's one claim to distinction was military: he fought well at Oudenarde, and was the last reigning King of England to lead troops into battle, which he did at Dettingen, in 1743, when he advanced on foot at the head of his infantry, and defeated the French. No-one could ever accuse George II of lacking courage.

George III 1760–1820

Born 1738
Crowned Westminster
Buried Windsor

George II's eldest son, Frederick, Prince of Wales, was unlike his father in many respects. A man of taste and intelligence, Frederick took a lively pleasure in society and an interest in politics. He may not have been a particularly strong character, but he appears in an attractive light, if only because of the extravagant persecution to which he was subjected by his father. 'Poor Fred' died in 1751, however, and the heir to the throne became his young son, George, who was aged 22 when he succeeded.

George III, unlike his two predecessors, was an English King rather than a German ruler and was proud to be so. Intensely patriotic, he 'gloried in the name of Briton'. Conventionally pious, he was a pattern of domestic virtue, the more strikingly in that both the preceding and the following generations of his family, in accordance with the spirit of the times, were conspicuously loose in their morals. Conscientious to a fault, he laboured hard and long at the bewildering political problems associated with the American and French Revolutions, and received little credit for his pains. Simple in his tastes, he loved farming and craftsmanship, and the company of his people.

Much of this, however, was a slow growth. The young George was pathetically insecure, and found the world of politics a hard place which offered little in the way of true friendship. The ministers whom he trusted, Bute and North, proved broken reeds. It took him a long time to learn that uncongenial company can provide the most reliable help,

as in the case of William Pitt the Younger.

The loss of the American colonies, finalised by the Treaty of Versailles in 1783, was a sore trial for George, who was widely, and quite unfairly, regarded as responsible. By contrast, when war broke out with revolutionary France in 1793, George became the symbol of national pride, and the monarchy rose in esteem to a pitch not known since Stuart days.

From middle life onwards, George suffered from bouts of illness which affected him both mentally and physically. His condition has since been diagnosed as *porphyria*, a genetically-caused condition. For the last ten years of his long reign, therefore, the King was tragically and irredeemably insane.

George IV 1820–1830

Born 1762
Crowned Westminster
Buried Windsor

Whatever respect George III gained for the monarchy was eroded by his eldest son. George IV acted as Regent during his father's madness, and then succeeded to the throne in 1820. Compulsively vain, spendthrift and frivolous, he showed himself unreliable – though frequently infatuated – both in love and politics. His domestic affairs were the scandal of the nation, and his petty intrigues constantly impeded the business of government.

He considered himself a connoisseur of style, and employed architects, interior decorators and tailors

OPPOSITE: *George I, first sovereign of the House of Hanover. He was not a popular king as he spoke little English and preferred to live in his native Hanover.* LEFT: *George II, whose reign marked the last time that an English king led his troops into battle.*

BELOW LEFT: *George III, who became the symbol of national pride when war broke out with the French in 1793. The King continued to win affection and respect. His taste for simple country pleasures – he was known as 'Farmer George' – endeared him to his people.*

on a stupendous scale (at least, the resultant debts were stupendous). His favourite architect was John Nash, the master of stucco illusion, and the creator of the Brighton Pavilion. Much of George's life was spent in creating or pursuing illusions. Towards the end of his life, he was said to have convinced himself that he charged with the British cavalry down the slope at Waterloo: 'Very steep, your Majesty', commented the Duke of Wellington.

RIGHT: *George IV in coronation robes, by Sir Thomas Lawrence. The King's coronation procession and banquet were probably the most splendid ever staged in Britain.*

William IV 1830–1837

Born 1765
Crowned Westminster
Buried Windsor

George IV was succeeded by his brother William, who had served in the Navy and was widely known as 'the Sailor King'. Less flatteringly, he was also dubbed 'Silly Billy', for his shortcomings of tact, judgement and intellect. From 1790 to 1811 he had lived in regular if unmarried bliss with an actress, Mrs Jordan, who bore him ten children. In 1818 he married a German princess, for dynastic reasons but they had only two sickly daughters, who died early.

William's politics are best described as obstructionist. He had been a Whig when his father's governments were Tory, he was a Tory when his own ministers were Whigs. His grudging acceptance of the Reform Act 1832 indicated the difficulties that the monarchy was having in coming to terms with the pressures of the early modern age.

William IV, who spent the early years of his life at sea, became popularly known as the 'Sailor King'. He served in the West Indies under Nelson. He had no surviving children and it was his late brother's daughter, Princess Victoria, who succeeded to the throne.

Victoria 1837–1901

Born 1819
Crowned Westminster
Buried Frogmore

By the late 1830s the monarchy was beginning to look a disreputable and even unnecessary institution. Kings were no longer expected to rule, only to reign. And when they reigned as badly as George IV or William IV, it began to be debatable whether they were necessary at all.

From this low point the monarchy was rescued by Queen Victoria, one of the most notable figures in British royal history. Her achievement was to restore respect and usefulness to the Crown, and then to go further by becoming (like Elizabeth I or Henry V or Edward I before her) the incarnate spirit of the nation, the symbol of its identity and its will.

This achievement was not a sudden occurrence. The young Victoria was the unlikely product of the belated marriage of one of William IV's brothers, the Duke of Kent. A lively, pleasure-loving princess, she showed plenty of signs of her Hanoverian heredity. Marriage to an admirable, if sometimes slightly too-good-to-be-true German prince, Albert of Saxe-Coburg-Gotha, sobered her and gave her a genuine sense of responsibility.

Her early widowhood – Albert died of typhoid fever in 1861 – devastated her, and sent her into a retirement from which she only gradually emerged. In the last twenty years of her reign, however, she became as completely loved and idolised as Elizabeth I had been, and over an inconceivably vaster empire.

Part of the secret of Victoria's success was her ability to mingle shrewd commonsense with awesomely high principles. She revered the ideal of family life, but was robustly practical about the tiresomeness of small children. This mixture of realism with idealism was peculiarly appropriate to an age which was daily extending the scope of human capacity, through science, industry and exploration, and which was at the same time facing frightening problems of its own creation.

Victoria's other great asset as a monarch was her relative ordinariness. In a period when middle-

OPPOSITE: *Queen Victoria, whose reign spanned the growth of the Empire, represented the continuity and stability of the British way of life. From a state portrait, 1859.*
RIGHT: *George V, first sovereign of the House of Windsor, portrayed in Garter regalia. George was a benign and dutiful king.*

class values were paramount, she embodied the qualities that the middle classes most admired – devotion to family and friends, frugality, conscientious discharge of duties, integrity and reliability. Everything in short that was summed up in the word 'respectability'. It was a concept that meant more in nineteenth-century England, than it does now. So when her soldiers saluted Victoria's name on the far frontiers of her ever-expanding empire, it was no empty gesture: she was, very specially, *their* Queen.

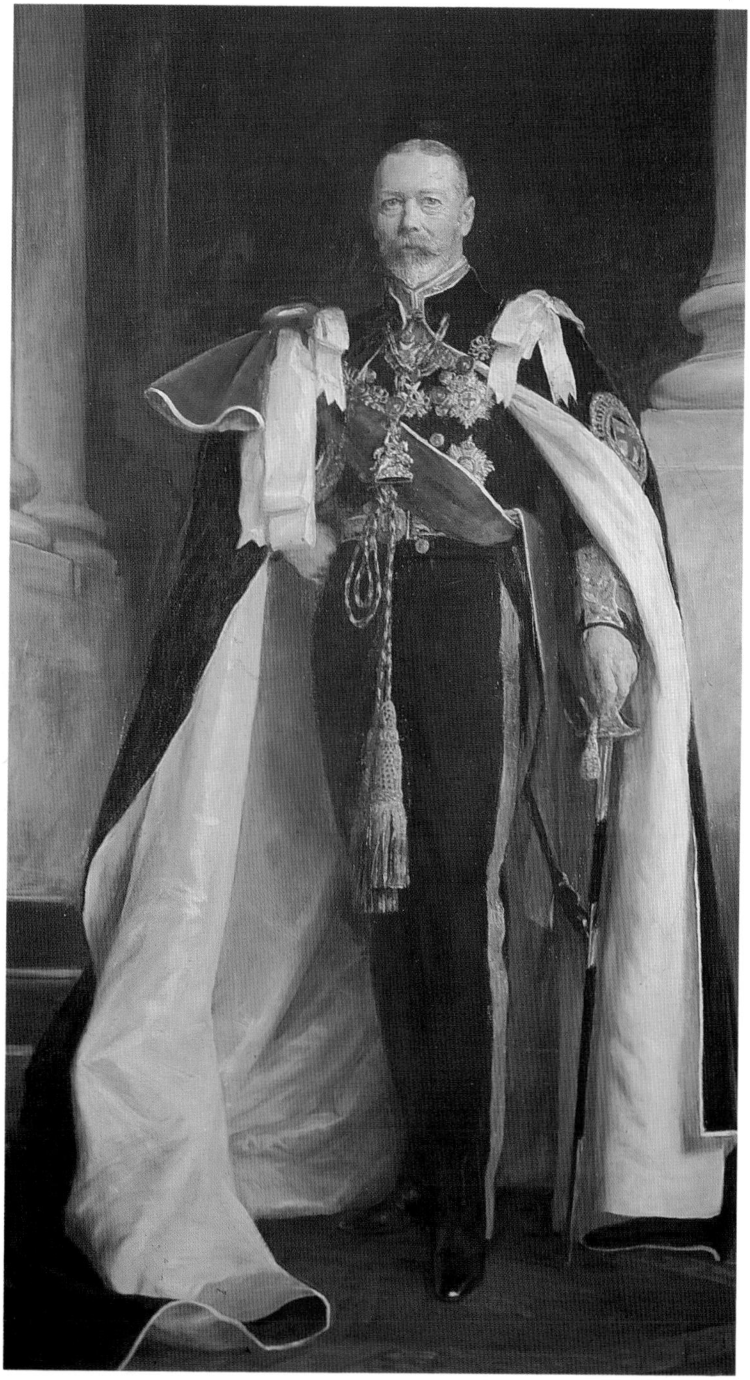

Edward VII 1901–1910

Born 1841
Crowned Westminster
Buried Windsor

Queen Victoria's eldest son had to endure a prolonged apprenticeship, in the course of which he was not given a great deal to do. He did not always bear his enforced idleness as well as his mother would have liked, but in the absence of a job it is hardly surprising that he chose to engage himself in the pleasures of smart society.

As King, he showed a talent for stateliness that sat well on the monarch of the greatest empire that the world had ever seen and, in more practical vein, he played a genuine enabling role in the diplomacy that led to the construction of the Triple Entente of England, France and Italy.

George V 1910–1936

Born 1865
Crowned Westminster
Buried Windsor

Edward VII's eldest son, Albert, died at the age of 28, and it was his second son, George, who succeeded him. There was something of both George I and George II about the severe and military formality of George V, but he had been brought up in the Victorian tradition and never faltered in his devotion to duty.

His reign was dominated by the horrors of the First World War. It was none of the King's making, and he had to act as figurehead for the national will in harrowing circumstances – a role he performed with impeccable dignity. He was haunted ever afterwards by the death of his cousin, Nicholas, Tsar of Russia.

After the War, amid the shifting tides of the 1920s and 1930s, the Crown stood for continuity and stability in a way that was all the more valued for not being overstated. King George V was an admirable 'institutional monarch'.

Edward VIII, later Duke of Windsor, who renounced his kingship when difficulties arose over his intention to marry Mrs Wallis Simpson. There was popular feeling for Edward VIII during the Abdication crisis but it soon faded after the accession of George VI.

Edward VIII   1936

Born 1894
Uncrowned
Buried Frogmore

King George V's eldest son almost reversed his father's qualities. Edward was full of charm, easily moved to emotion, informal and approachable. However, he lacked steadiness, strength of will and sense of duty. As Prince of Wales he showed concern for the plight of the poor and unemployed (his protest, 'Something must be done,' pricked minds that would have been immune to more serious proposals). At the same time he led a glittering set of international socialites. Always susceptible, he lost his heart at a critical moment to an American divorcée, Mrs Wallis Simpson.

When told that marriage to Mrs Simpson would be unacceptable to a great majority of his subjects, he preferred to abdicate. He was subsequently created Duke of Windsor, served during the war years as Governor of the Bahamas, and spent the rest of his life in retirement in Paris, where he died in 1972.

George VI   1936–1952

Born 1895
Crowned Westminster
Buried Windsor

The Duke of York, second son of George V, had never expected or wished to succeed to the throne, and his brother's abdication cast a burden which weighed on him more heavily than it might have done on others. He was naturally diffident and anxious, and suffered from a speech impediment. But he never lacked bravery or enterprise. He had fought as a young naval officer at Jutland, and was the first member of the Royal Family to learn to fly; and his sense of duty was invincible. Fortified by the influence of his Queen, who swiftly acquired immense popularity in her own right (leading her to become a legend in her lifetime), King George coped with the aftermath of the Abdication in a way that quickly restored confidence in the monarchy.

When the horrors of the Second World War descended shortly afterwards on Britain, and on London in particular, the royal couple rose superbly to the occasion. King George VI and Queen Elizabeth stayed at what they and their subjects saw as their posts all through the Blitz, and showed love and care for their people in gestures that stilled the meanest critics. Their daughters served in uniform, and the identification of the Royal Family with the national will was complete.

The effort, however, was crushing and the King's health was permanently affected. He died, rather suddenly, in the winter of 1952.

BELOW: *The coronation of George VI. The great day was marked by solemn pageantry. The King had to restore confidence in the monarchy after the Abdication. From a painting by Frank Salisbury.* OPPOSITE: *Her Majesty Queen Elizabeth II, from the state portrait by James Gunn.*

Born 1926
Crowned Westminster

The reign of Queen Elizabeth II since 1952 has spanned a period of rapid and occasionally turbulent change. Britain's position in the world, her economy, and the very shape and structures of society have all been transformed and many traditional institutions have suffered in the process. Through all this, the path of the Crown has been marked out by The Queen herself, in a prolonged display of unwavering devotion to duty and quiet pragmatism which has met a nationally-felt need, and has won her the unstinting respect and affection of her peoples.

As hereditary head of state for Great Britain and Northern Ireland, The Queen has symbolic and formal functions and duties but no direct powers. She is an embodiment of national identity and continuity and, with her family, performs countless formalities to mark events in the lives of individuals and communities and provides valuable patronage for innumerable charities. This is a far cry from the powerful rule of Plantagenet, Tudor or Stuart monarchs, or even the busy, influential interventions of the Hanoverians. But it meets the nation's need for a social focus and, to some extent, separates pomp from power. Many would agree that Her Majesty is able to wield a significant degree of influence by virtue of her matchless experience, allied to great natural shrewdness.

The Queen's reign has seen the Commonwealth taking the place of the British Empire. In 1953, Queen Elizabeth II declared the 'Commonwealth ideal' as being 'an entirely new conception, built on the highest qualities of the spirit of man: friendship, loyalty and the desire for freedom and peace'. By 1966, almost all the Empire had gained independence and a vast majority of the new nations applied for membership of the Commonwealth. Today, 51 former British colonies are still joined in an alliance of voluntary co-operation and The Queen makes an official visit to a Commonwealth country at least once a year and receives reciprocal visits.

Elizabeth II is now the longest-reigning British monarch since Queen Victoria and The Queen's Silver

institution of the monarchy. However, the marriage broke down amid widely-publicised bitterness, and a divorce followed. These troubles, together with the divorces of Princess Anne and the Duke of York, were seen by some to diminish the monarchy in public esteem. The death of Diana, Princess of Wales on 31 August 1997 in a car crash in Paris unleashed a surge of intense public emotion which seemed to demand a greater warmth and more relaxed nature in social attitudes, reinforcing those who sought to reduce the monarchy's formality.

LEFT: *The Queen, in the robes of Sovereign of the Order of the Garter, arriving at St George's Chapel in Windsor for the annual ceremony.*

BELOW: *A portrait of Her Majesty The Queen wearing the Parliamentary Robe, painted by Richard Stone.*

Jubilee in 1977 was celebrated with enthusiasm and great displays of loyalty. The Crown seemed happily poised in public esteem, and, if old habits of deference had already waned, there was plenty of solidly won respect to compensate. The years since 1978, however, saw the position of the monarchy disturbed by both personal and institutional developments.

Supported by Prince Philip, Duke of Edinburgh, to whom she was married on 20 November 1947, The Queen is head of a large family. The first child of the royal marriage and the current heir to the throne is Prince Charles, the Prince of Wales, who was born on 14 November 1948 and was invested as Prince of Wales at Caernarvon Castle on 1 July 1969. He married Lady Diana Spencer on 29 July 1981; two sons were born to the marriage – Prince William, born 21 June 1982 and Prince Henry, born 15 September 1984. At first, this seemed to be a fairy-tale romance and the beginning of a new era of enthusiasm for the Royal Family and the